DEVI'S DISCIPLES

INDONESIAN WOMEN POETS

EDITED BY
INTAN PARAMADITHA

TILTED AXIS PRESS 2020
THANKS TO OUR KICKSTARTER BACKERS

DEVIANT DISCIPLES: FEMINIST RESISTANCE IN INDONESIAN POETRY

The famous Balinese tale of Calon Arang, a powerful witch who lived during the reign of King Erlangga in the 11th century, is preserved through literature, arts, and performances in Indonesia. The widow Calon Arang is furious because no one wants to marry her daughter, so she prays to Goddess Durga and asks her permission to spread disease and death in the village. A threat to the kingdom and powerful men, Calon Arang reveals a deep-seated fear in society when a woman holds so much power. Another intriguing aspect of the legend is the seven female students of Calon Arang. Each has a name and a grotesque look. With sharp teeth, tusks, and long fiery tongues, they dance over corpses and cooperate to assist their teacher to take revenge. Calon Arang teaches and organises, and her relationship with her disciples expose another kind of horror: the fear of subversive potentials when women unite, collaborate, and transfer their knowledge to other women.

The title *Deviant Disciples* is taken from Toeti Heraty's poem in this slim collection, "Entreating the Goddess Durga," excerpted from her long prose poem *Calon Arang: A Sacrificial Victim of the Patriarchy* published in 2000. A rewriting of the Balinese witch story with a feminist framework, Heraty's *Calon Arang* can be seen as a representative of the bold and rebellious ways in which Indonesian women poets use words to challenge patriarchal language, religion, and culture. I use the phrase "Deviant Disciples" to highlight collaboration and exchange of knowledge among women to interrogate power structures. These aspects, I hope, align with the spirit of *Translating Feminisms,* a series of chapbooks initiated by Tilted Axis Press to promote women writers and feminist thoughts in Asia. I am proud to present this selection of poems by Indonesian women writers as part of the *Translating Feminisms* series, and to situate our collaboration in the larger landscape where women work collectively to decolonise global literature and challenge the singular notion of feminism.

Deviant Disciples features five prominent Indonesian women poets. Selecting the poets and their works for a chapbook was a challenging task; geographical location was a major consideration, particularly with regards to the dominant position of Jakarta and the hegemony of the Javanese culture resulting from the legacy of the authoritarian regime's cultural politics. Raised in the capital city, I am aware that being in the centre provided me with the privilege of access, networks, and visibility. While my selection still cannot be free from geographical biases, this chapbook is an effort to present women poets of different generations and cultural backgrounds, from the legendary poet and philosophy professor Toeti Heraty (b. 1933), who first published her poetry collection in 1974, to Shinta Febriany (b. 1979), a poet and theatre director of the younger generation who writes poetry and produces performances in her hometown Makassar. Magelang-based Dorothea Rosa Herliany subverts the conventions of Indonesian language through her rebellious imagery and sentence structure; Hanna Fransisca engages with her Chinese heritage, myths, and the bleak reality of women in Singkawang, West Kalimantan. West-Sumatran born Zubaidah Djohar uses poetry to criticize the demonization of women's bodies and the implementation of the shariah law in Aceh.

In a larger volume I wish to include more women poets such as Gratiagusti Chananya Rompas, Cyntha Hariadi, and Ratri Ninditya, all of whom have portrayed the urban space in unique ways, reflecting on how multiple identities of women as mothers, lovers, and workers are negotiated in messy capitalist Jakarta. I also wish to include deceased women poets forgotten by the Indonesian literary canon, such as Rukiah, and emerging talents, such as Fitri Nganthi Wani, daughter of disappeared poet Widji Thukul, who writes about the memory of her father as a victim of Suharto's dictatorship as well as her own views as a young woman shaped by a different historical context. For those who are interested in exploring more poems by Indonesian women writers, *Rainbow: 18 Indonesian Women Poets* edited by Toeti Heraty (Indonesia Tera: 2008) is an excellent anthology, showcasing works by well-acclaimed poets including Oka Rusmini, Cok Sawitri, and Abidah El Khalieqy.

It is a delight to present five Indonesian women

poets and their bold voices through the brilliant translation of Tiffany Tsao, Norman Erikson Pasaribu, and Eliza Vitri Handayani. I decided to collaborate with these three author-translators due to their commitment to promoting Indonesian literature in translation, particularly works by authors concerned with feminist and queer issues, authors from underrepresented backgrounds, and authors who do not receive much attention or support in the Indonesian literary scene. Tiffany Tsao is the former Indonesia-at-Large editor for *Asymptote*. With Norman Erikson Pasaribu, she edited a series showcasing Indonesian literature in cooperation with Ubud Writers and Readers Festival. Most of the authors highlighted are women, including novelists Ratih Kumala and Dewi Kharisma Michellia as well as poets Gratiagusti Chananya Rompas and Cyntha Hariadi. Eliza Vitri Handayani, on the other hand, is the founder of InterSastra, an independent platform for literary and artistic exploration. It promotes literary translation through translation workshops, seminars, and author showcases. The most recent publication of InterSastra is the *Unrepressed* series, for which Tiffany Tsao is the translation editor, and it features works by writers whose experiences and identities are considered under-represented.

Toeti Heraty's "Entreating the Goddess Durga," the first poem in this collection, introduces the deviant spirit in many of the poems selected here. The story of the powerful widow *Calon Arang* has been reinterpreted by many (male) writers and artists, but Heraty's version was the first that reframes the story with a strong feminist perspective. Heraty focuses on the difficulty of being an old widow in the Balinese/Indonesian society, her loneliness and sense of being wasted, and how the future of her daughter becomes her only source of happiness. Linking the legend to contemporary gender politics, *Calon Arang* underlines how patriarchal power, represented by the king and the priest in the story, is threatened by the presence of a powerful woman. As a feminist icon, Heraty has often been seen by readers as 'an angry feminist.' However, while Calon Arang is about the witch's wrath, her other poems can be funny and playful yet they remain incisive of women's position in society. "A Middle-Aged Ballad," another poem in this chapbook, tells the story of a woman's search for fleeting happiness at an age when youth and opportunities have departed.

Another celebrated poet, Dorothea Rosa

Herliany, came from a generation that emerged in the 1980s during the Suharto regime. Her poetry collection, *Kill The Radio,* was published in the UK in 2007, and her poems have been translated and published in several countries. Herliany was known for her feminist themes and her experimentation with language. Formal Indonesian language during the New Order, known for its heavy use of euphemism, was a tool to regulate society, preserve stability, and conceal traces of violence. This linguistic politics results in a hypocritical society, one that Herliany attacks with her bold and unrestrained language. She violates grammatical conventions, a tendency that Tiffany Tsao attempts to capture through her translation ("i arrive who knows where. a circlingcircling / in a labyrinth. the longest of all journeys but / sansmap") to rebel against societal conventions. She speaks of desire and pleasure through dark imagery ("your body crawling with wormsandworms") and violent gestures ("stabbing" and "ripping"). Alluding to the bible and the Indian epics, Herliany attacks myths of feminine purity and loyalty and challenges the Suharto ideology of *Ibu*ism (mother-ism), which emphasises women's subservient qualities as mothers and wives. Like Toeti Heraty's Calon Arang,

Herliany's women can be wild ("give me explosionsexplosions and a bed creaking in a strange new way") or monstrous ("now i drench my body, in black blood"), asserting their agency by reclaiming their voices and bodies.

Zubaidah Djohar is a poet, researcher, and human rights activist who often speaks about transformation in Aceh, the implementation of shariah law, and the marginalisation of women due to politics and religious practice. Her poems are often based on actual events, written in a poignant and straightforward manner, and she often proposes an interpretation of Islamic texts to challenge the dominant patriarchal narrative. In "In The Land of 7000 Skirts, I," Djohar criticises the policy in West Aceh to give 7000 skirts to police women's bodies by making sure that women dress modestly to avoid sexual violence. In "Siti Khalwat," she writes about the abuse of a woman accused of having extra-marital sex under the *sharia* law. She points out not only the presence of state terrorism through the moral police and discriminatory policies but also violence involved in the 'social courts' set up by members of the community to judge others. In a climate that gives birth to witch-hunting and self-righteousness, women suffer the most as their bodies are vilified, tortured, and humiliated.

The link between body and politics is also explored by poet Shinta Febriany, who is also known as one of the few women playwrights and theatre directors in Indonesia today. With Kala Teater, a Makassar-based theatre group she founded in 2006, she has staged performances with themes ranging from sexual violence to urban issues and environmental problems. Similar to her performances, Febriany's poems often deploy provocative and discordant images to question gender roles. In "open body," she alludes to the figure of Mary Magdalene and her seven demons to speak about the vilification of women who do not fit societal expectations. Similar to Zubaidah Djohar, Febriany problematises how the society easily judges and marks certain (female bodies) as dirty and sinful. She also writes about distrust and anger towards the state, themes that characterise the works of many poets who witnessed the beginning of the new *Reformasi* (political reform) era in 1998. In "nightmare from the state," she describes the country as "the vastest prison," arguing that the state has not changed so much even after the *reformasi,* as "the stench invades the air," "nightmares keep coming," and "the people have felt betrayed."

The last poet featured in this collection is Hanna Fransisca, who explores Chinese-Indonesian identity and the violence of the Indonesian state through unusual, often disturbing imagery. At first glance, the portrayal of her Chinese cultural heritage as a native of Singkawang seems to evoke nostalgia, yet the idyllic is always haunted by the tragic or the sadistic. Amidst the memories of temples, mountains, and spirits, women in Singkawang are waiting for marriage that will bring them to Singapore or Taiwan, objectified as commodities: "Slanted eyes for your carnal needs." Fransisca's poems are full of uneasy juxtapositions. Just as she mixes the imagery of rich Chinese culture with the corrupt and the rotten, she juxtaposes food and gore to talk about desire and decay, dream and death. In "A Chinese Song," she brings us "naked white chicken roasting in a cauldron," evoking the smell of spices, and the image of the chicken is interchangeable with a young woman and "the river of blood." She cleverly plays with the name of the woman, Dara, which means 'girl' and 'dove,' both regarded as "a special dish." Violence against Chinese-Indonesian women is a prevalent theme in Fransisca's poems. In "May Poem," we are immediately reminded of the May 1998 riot, in which many Chinese women became victims of rape and murder. The story of people burned to death becomes corporeal, and it implicates us: "You're free to chew the dead's skin and flesh."

The works of Indonesian women poets demonstrate the powerful ways in which feminist resistance has been articulated in the non-Western World. Their poems can be playful or angry, but all of them are fearless. The poets featured in this collection can be seen as "deviant disciples" of Calon Arang, a smart and powerful woman figure who threatens patriarchal order. Like Calon Arang's black magic, language for these women poets has become a tool to critique, reinterpret, and disobey.

POEMS BY TOETI HERATY

translated by Tiffany Tsao

ENTREATING THE GODDESS DURGA

An excerpt from *Calon Arang: a sacrificial victim of the patriarchy*

A widowed woman is one no longer beloved
between a love-struck virgin, and a weeping wife
    bereft
is a cliff of disparity—a widow
lying in bed, a heartbeat of emptiness
pulsing in her vagina, a bolster in her arms;
this is what the seething Calon Arang must endure.

Over time she finds solace in her daughter's beauty
too late for the mother, but they'll court the
    daughter
yet not a single suitor shows up; whether
it's them or her, who knows, nonetheless
she seeks permission from the goddess Durga
to destroy them, her neighbours. To this end,
    every night
to the graveyard she goes, bearing offerings of bits
from bodies, even decking herself out in organs:

'Sure thing,' says the goddess

'but only the villages and outskirts
leave the city folk untouched.'
So there, among the graves, garlanded in guts
earringed in lungs, she washes her hair in fresh blood
and dances round, and initiates her acolytes;
disease sweeps through the locals, who snuff it after
fever and chills; weeping breaks out
across the land; the king's authority is shaken
from his seat on the throne; he calls
the whole lot to the palace (meaning most likely,
all the cabinet ministers, maybe the army too);
the top troops are dispatched, the equivalent of
today's special forces, but they're wiped out, no match
for the dark arts of the Dirah widow.

Calon Arang, a.k.a. the great Rangda,
and her deviant disciples: Weksirsa and Mahi-sawandana
Lendya, Lende, and Lindi; Guyang, Larung, and Gandi,
all stepping in line with the woman from Dirah.

Though I must admit as I survey this scene,

I'm impressed by its sheer creativity;
this convincing legend screams 'projection'.
Projected, specifically, by power-thirsty men
brimming with loathing and vengefulness
towards women, but also,
fear.

A MIDDLE-AGED BALLAD

In Kampung Bali, within a motel
made respectable by the appellation 'Wisma'
sits a woman in her middle age, waiting for her lover
the room is cheap and the air is stale
with an electric fan in perpetual stall
the bathroom has a mould problem, but at least the water runs clear
a plastic yellow gayung near the toilet
a bed on a wooden base of blue
on the dust-coated walls is scrawled in pen
'Romeo and Julia', and beneath, 'Cicih dan Iman'
heart skewered by crisscrossed arrows

It's not the waiting—, what bothers her
or offends her, to be more exact
is the owner who dared to wonder out loud
as he watched her climbing up the stairs:
"get a load of this hooker
what's the rush
putting on airs
but look at her blush"
street sounds waft in: the sputter
of passing bajaj, the cries of a meatball vendor and tinker

drifting up and through the window:
a granny swearing, her washing on the line
muddied by kids playing outside

No, not the waiting—, though he's taking his time
what could be keeping him, she sits, then lies
on the bed, a pillow in her anxious embrace
trying to keep all the thoughts at bay:
"darling – you know I want you, I need you
please don't ever betray my trust
even if betraying your wife
is something you do all the time—
we've been together for so long
I'm not just some girl—all I want is to taste
a drop of life's sweetness, it's at least
my right to hope for that much"

Don't tell me—he came to his senses
and decided to go home to his wife
for isn't there that side to consider:
"haven't I been faithful all these years
raising our kids, working by your side
to support our family, we've paid all our debts
I get along with your folks pretty well
even though your siblings are a useless bunch
every Sunday, every Lebaran
every selamatan, every arisan

an occasional movie with just us two, gossiping
about neighbors, aren't these also the ties that
   bind..."

"what exactly am I waiting for
—I'm pathetic—, I bet he's gone back to his wife
what am I hoping for even, it isn't right
to wait for someone else's husband—"

The door creaks open and he enters,
suitcase in hand, there is no more delay
all counter arguments fall to the wayside
no chit-chat required, kisses and hugs
are a waste of time, for the very same bed
that a moment ago was a continent stretching
from the north pole to antarctica
is now traversed by two middle-aged creatures
amidst dust and grime, mute witnesses
whose lips partake of honey—, of living
that is past its youth, that has suffered
wounds, each stroking the other, kissing away
the scars from sharp weapons and thorns,
and all the gashes left by life
an hour or two is potent enough
to heal—

But of course

before they know it
someone knocks at the door:
"here's your change
from the payment for the room
we'll be back with the towels
want to order some drinks?"

POEMS BY DOROTHEA ROSA HERLIANY

Translated by Tiffany Tsao

MARRIAGE OF THE KNIFE

i arrive who knows where. a circlingcircling
in a labyrinth. the longest of all journeys but
sansmap. here in the purest shade of pitch
black. i grope down an alley between a river
and ravine.

theres a scream, songlike. from
my own lips, i bet. i hear a groan,
lullabylike. from my own lips, i bet.

but ive reached a land of the purest
alienation: your   body   crawling   with
    wormsandworms
which i ignore. until i consummate my pleasure.
before I consummate you too, stabbing
your heart, ripping your dick apart, all throbbing
in agony.

MARRIAGE OF THE BODILESS WHORE

you take me to a strange hill: the wandering of a sun
spreading the fragrance of sweat from Golgotha. death and
resurrection: ecstatic release from the trek of letter and tome.

"yeshua, youve mapped out the bliss of quest and pilgrimage.
the centurylong journeys among prayers and psalms un-
uttered. i seek the map and spell out a route that vanishes
in my palm and the prophets' words."

im just a whore with no heaven. dragging my body
allabout. offering contortions of hollowness and
fablesandfables of love. inside a stanza of panting and sweating.
a howling wolf. a nighttime revenge between shivers of
fear at allthewildbeasts.

i carry my heart between the hollows of a love

beyond disheveled. offering it to every man who paints their eyes in gusts of wind.

"yeshua, give me the bliss of strange new love.
give me explosionsexplosions and a bed creaking
   in a strange new way
give me all things that men don't own.
oh, not heaven, though!"

I crawl through whoknowswhat hills. all is empty
between the hollows of wind and words. between
   the murmurs
of those reading verseafterverse on angels and the
   tolling of
bellsbells. im just a whore wary of searching for
   doors
and the creaking of pews between prayers.

just a whore everplying sin, but i keep a stash
between versesandverses that remain unread,
   seeking
a clearing and tilling the hills. planting seeds of
   sweat and shudders
of wounds which will sprout into a garden of roses.

so you men! sneer when you're not in my arms!

SINTA'S ELEGY

i'm the sinta who called off her immolation.
meant to preserve bloodline purity
for rama, that king of cowards.
now i drench my body, in black blood.
to warm my ardor.
it sprouts in fields of defilement—the most sordid
    kind.

i track down rahwana,
and ask him to ravish me
into the void of the sky.
i let myself soar, beyond arm's
reach of that chicken-hearted loser.

who says my love is white? maybe grey,
or even the same dark shade as my life.
but listen to my melodious whinny.
incinerating everything holy and eternal.

i seize my life, not in fire
—that home for sinners.
but in solitude, futile and fallen.
to free my history of cowards
and liars. like that rama …

POEMS OF ZUBAIDAH DJOHAR

Translated by Norman Erikson Pasaribu

SITI KHALWAT: AN EXCERPT[1]

1.

find no uncertainties: the night's
neck-choking chronicle continues
inside of me.

I mean
how can I forget
when my body keeps
dancing a slit / a splinter /
of a witnessing / of an archiving /

---

[1] Khalwat is an Arabic (or at least a version of Arabic used in Indonesia) word to describe an encounter between a man and a woman in a place where there is no one is around (to witness that no sexual activities outside marriage are committed). In many cases, people accused of conducting khalwat will be punished not only by the legal moral police (wilayatul hisbah) but also by members of the community who create their own court. As there are no certainties in how we should define khalwat, numerous people have become victims of this social court, especially women, who have always been marginalized by the local practice of Islamic Sharia in Aceh. (A version of) Islamic Sharia was practiced in Aceh as mandated in four local regulations: Qanun 11 of 2002, Qanun 12 of 2003, Qanun 13 of 2003, Qanun 14 of 2003. The latter qanun ruled specifically about khalwat.

for the spiteful bruise
and how it jumps here
and here!
for the rabidness possessing
as a holy flag
stands still
on the groins
of the hypocrites!

see for yourself
how can I forget?
the commotion in
the front yard. how it
thunders in my heart
makes me think
of horses
and their whinny sex

hand us the woman!
    she is not here
oh, bullshit!
you, go search this place

and like a pack of hungry wolves
they sniff me out
they find me on my bed
they sever me from my daughter

who is asleep

the bitch is here![2]
so easily they make me
a lost kite
rolling up my hair to an iron arm
landing a punch on my back
and then another
I keep falling
and falling. I am
a broken twig, inside
their furious fists

and yet, still hungry
they throw me
into the mud
from the sewer

I lose all my color
I can see nothing
I can feel my odor bursting
out, reaching
to the margin of this pursuit

---

2 A sentence used by a man when the people in a kampong in Aceh were looking for a woman suspected of doing khalwat, as reported by the Woman and Adat Law research in 2009.

they cast me out to a soccer field
(but isn't it a garden of Eden
for them, the hundreds of eyes corralling,
as I am the Eve, as I am the utterly naked one)

and so ready they are
to jump on me!

so this is the woman
haha, it makes sense now, why he
left the other woman: who is mere wrinkles
and shabby nightgowns

some of them come to me
gnaw and gnaw on my flesh
my body throbs and trembles
it turns red, bleeding dark lava:
how it refuses to pour out blood!

cut her goddamn hair![3]
shout some men behind me
and, as if in a race, they run
around to borrow scissors
I bet she'll look better now
bruised face goes best with bald head

---

3 One suggestion from a man, during a khalwat prosecution.

such a visual diversion
and still an unfair diversion for me!

and a mousy man approaches
he kicks me twice on the thigh
and just like that he shears me
and leaves just a centimeter
of thornlike hair

as if in a dream
faintly I can hear
the sound of my love,
the man who was with me
during the rainy days

You!
My love!
Where have you been?
I've been here for three hours now. See
how these men erect a judgement day
for me! See how in this false court, I
am alone: no verses defending me
no smoke and prayer that will cure my wound.

well, I will put things in your hand since
I have nothing to do with this
right, right. you better go back home now

when we got her, you weren't not with her / she was alone /
you are free to go. you're not guilty
and... I can tell you just got back from fishing
you reek of the sea, man, so salty. go now, have some rest.

almost like I stand before
two big mountains
rulers of the island
loud and thundering!

and my body: it's throbbing, trembling
but not because of fear / I am not afraid
not because I am alone / even though, yes, I am alone

But you!
My dear love!
How can you forget
the nights our eyes sung
to each other
our souls danced around
the heavenly shore
when nobody else was around

the silence

of our gathering

look what has become
of those eyes now?
Black-bagged,
they are no longer
the eyes
that made your days fleeting:
swallowing every one of your daydreams
feeding you with hopes

and this bosom, now painted all over
with grave flowers
wasn't it once so surging
it could sail our ship to a whirlpool
of desire?

and this ruin of a hip
wasn't it once the most picturesque
kettledrum
where all of your ice
erupted?

and look!
this sharpening crown
of thorns on my head
wasn't it (only yesterday)

a shimmering seine
that keeps curling and unraveling
wasn't it a curtain
where you went into hiding,
where you spied
on the rustling wind?

but whatever
go back to your night bed
you are a house cat, you rob your master
of her flesh
you are a forest snake, and now you are full
you need to hibernate

I will be here
inside the blue / being the blue / going into the blue
and this ghost-face on me
will not vanish / will not be a prey for these parasites:
these self-venerating gods / these so-called purities!

I have the strength / I can look them in the eyes
with all my bones crushed / swallowed by their judgment day
I am alive
I am alive

for a long, long prayer
asking for justice.

HERE ON THE LAND OF 7000 SKIRTS, I

Here on the land of 7000 skirts, I settle
pouring love to the Lord, taking care of my family
because divine devotion is not just a late-night Tahajjud
but also giving your heart to the people of the land

Here on the land of 7000 long skirts, I gather up my thoughts
the ceiling tells me a story of bodies in prison
nothing can escape the untamable gaze, they said / not even the body, they said
so body brings decay to the land / so body summons the punishments from above

But, men of the fences / how dare you forget?
your heads father the gaze / and from your terrible hands
the ravage keeps streaming / why do you suffocate our bodies
just so you can say Islam is at the heart of this land?

Here on the land where you ordered 7000 skirts, I am caught

by white walls against me / faces of women, the corpse candidates,
printed on my shadow / crestfallen, with their days numb / ered
and this place, horribly doctorless, is now an open-mouth cemetery
the never-born babies line up / to jump into their graves
(and none of this will happen, if you don't lose your nurani!)

Here on the land of 7000 skirts, I stop
to look sharply at your face
have you wondered about the smell?
the skirts you put on us / have thorns all over
now they are smudged with women's blood / our blood
and you scrape it on the wall to draw a holy symbol!
and do you see the shabbiness, the faintness of these white rooms?
the people inside, so wilted and dull!
have you traced the steps of tsunami
and the political conflict
on our body?
We have wounds so corroded / and they ask for a splash of peace
and have you seen how dirtily dreadful your land

has become?
it begs for a generous mind-heart:
the sharia-beads of your Lord, who is also my Lord

Here on the land of 7000 skirts, I stop
asking you all, men of the fences
what is the sharia that guides your story?
because the Lord is merciful
She kindly asks us to rethink things with our heart
She forbids us to crack-break the Earth
but here on the land of 7000 skirts, I stop
asking you one more time,
"Which of the favors of your Lord that you've denied?
Hasn't the face of your land beamed with a piece of peace?"
Go seed your heart to the ground, see how it'll lose its pitch-blackness
a sharp mind and heart bring joys to the land, I'd say
but not your sea of skirts

But here on the land of 7000 skirts, I come to a stop
witnessing how it's no longer 7000
from dozens to ten thousands, stretching north to south

imagine thousands of souls torn apart
thousands of bodies ripped apart
Happy fasting to you who govern this land
I know Ramadhan will be a room with a mirror

"7000 skirts" is a 2009 campaign of the regent of West Aceh district to push for the regulation for women to wear Muslim dress. In January 2010, he announced that women were forbidden to wear trousers. The West Aceh administration prepared 7000 skirts to be distributed to women. Women who wore tight outfits were sanctioned and given free skirts. Some of them faced sexual harassment.

POEMS OF SHINTA FEBRIANY

Translated by Eliza Vitri Handayani

OPEN BODY

your friends left
when they found out you are not a saint.

you are a tragedy
a regretted conversation
a scene they wish to erase
from reality.

your friends gossip to the wind
about the man who visited your body,
releasing his desires, paying off his pains.

you stand naked before the mirror
looking into your wretched heart.
you look for the seven demons in your body
but you can't find them.

there is no one in your body.
jesus doesn't need to exorcise anyone.

you embrace your open body
that is adept at facing
the desires that besiege you
in the dark and in the light.

my body is ready
for all kinds of weather.
this is a body that can always be shared.

you rave by yourself.
while staring at a highway
that seems hopeless.

there are no dogs on the highway.
there are no dogs dying
of thirst.
you don't have to take well water
with a shawl and wooden shoes.

maybe I am the dog
that your religion tells you.
the hungry and thirsty dog
that fails to die
as it must remember its shame.

you're raving again.
your friends have left
you alone
and you are heartbroken

did mary magdalene hurt as much as I do?

your question leaves an echo.

before the wooden cross you kneel,
and speak to your father in heaven:

I want to kiss my friends' lips
who call my body dirty,
an insult to propriety.
my body is not a marker of sin.
bless me, father.

you breathe in the sadness in your body
until it fades,

until the shadows of your friends
disappear without a trace.

NIGHTMARE FROM THE STATE

people are waking up
as the stench invades the air,
opening doors and windows,
dust and rain scrambling in,
settling on nightgowns, blankets,
and the dingy dining table.

the whistle has been blown
everywhere, like sirens
blaring on the streets
igniting fear of living

thoughts are inflamed
bodies are killing themselves
and the state stands on the tower
calling for a fight.

nights are no longer holy
as the nightmares keep coming,
rioting against all hopes.
like the posters of politicians
who wish to be loved
but the people have felt betrayed.

like you,

on the fateful morning
when you couldn't find
your lover in bed.

your lover had left,
leaving a sentence on the vanity mirror:
this country no longer loves me!

sadness breaks into your heart.
glasses of water
pass through your desert throat.

you watch the news on tv that says
that the country has been wounded
by gangs of robbers
who pretended to love her.

but you don't feel sorry.
you whisper to the quiet around you:
I no longer believe in this country!

then a knock at the door calls for you.
a letter from your lover arrives so promptly:

my dear,
this country is the vastest prison
that forces us to breathe in its baseness

that does not protect us from darkness.
like the darkness of marsinah, satinah,
and other women.
I don't want to live
in a tattered country.

you imagine people
waving to the country
like your lover.

the morning stops feeling restless
sadness sprints
out of you.

POEMS BY HANNA FRANSISCA

Translated by Eliza Vitri Handayani

TAIWAN IN THE POOL OF MY EYES

: *Singkawang*

At Natuna the waves crash and scrape the salty shore
Upstream Roban, the bodies' fishy smell launches the boat
Sailing through the memories of Ci Kung Temple, moaning mountains,
Drifting foam, seeking for the wind spirit of Bengkayang.

At the mouth of the Singkawang River thousands of amois stare at the South China Sea
Looking for blue waves, amid pretty pieces of sunlight,
warm love that continues to wait.

The trees have always grown here, my love: fertility yields freshness,
twigs carrying lanterns,
piercing the eyes of the soul.

Ripples of water, ripples of the pool in mother's

eyes,
flow straight into the heart of heart.

To Singapore you go, in the Gulf of Taiwan you are confined.
Floating by the thousands, The Virgin Girl is chosen, is coveted: "Look here.
Look here, good Sir. Slanted eyes for your carnal needs,
strong muscles for your household chores. Hard workers hardly complaining.
Rough hands, rough lifelines. Singkawang is tourists' heaven, Sir.
Choose your match, take your girl across the sea.
Make Slanted Eyes your girlfriend,
They're good for more than one night,
Housewives for all the housework."

Blue ocean, open ocean, singing sorrowfully.
The pool of mother's tears, flowing straight into the heart of heart.

In Si Jangkung, in the Bougenvile Park, the petals fell forlorn
Poisoned air around the temple's yard, Mother's incensed prayer for those who suffer.
Ancestral spirits flying from Bengkayang, towards

   the Natuna Sea
to South China.

In the Heaven and Hell Temple, I return to my
   hometown. My footsteps now,
by writing this, are paid in full.

A CHINESE SONG

Naked white chicken roasting in a cauldron.
Sleep, ai, your slanted eyes are pinching dreams,
    long legs facing the sky,
creating yourself. A rainbow shawl
glides down
turns into fire.

Fine hairs, limp in the anxious light. A flash of
    passion
prompts her surrender. She puffs out her chest,
showing off fresh teenage meat. Spreading lust
between two thighs.

"What a beautiful open field. The smell of teenage
    hair and flesh,
like grass in the savanna. The horses run mightily,
crossing a dream
to the edges of nirvana."

The long neck stretches, a knife carves a valley
    dead center:
"The river of blood has stopped, Dara. Now sleep
as peacefully as an angel."

Dara's beauty is beyond compare. The smell of

fresh fur in the field.
Close your slanted eyes, my dear. You live in this country,
plant your sweat and do not dream.

Body caressed, eyes closed. The lines of death find longing.
A rainbow falls from the sky, Dara falls asleep basking in the fire. Warm love
radiates, from a pair of thighs
up to the head.

She is stretched out, spreading her wings
left and right. No, not to fly, my dear:
but to float on the dining table. To lay down on the spread of clinking plates,
sliced by the sheen of spoons, sharp knives, and the smell of palm wine. Dara is drunk and soaked in wine.
Soy sauce drips on her thighs. Vinegar acid
flushes her chest.

Oh such a lustful body,
fresh flesh lighting up the lush land, songs of young teenage girls!
Slanted eyes bright marble skin, studded with garlic and shallot. Warm pepper

Translating Feminisms

roasted by fire, salt and sugar:
smothering love without a sound.

Everything that lives needs to feel.
Everything that dies needs no form.

Is that you, Dara? The song dies, the voice is gone.
As you are born
as a special dish.

MAY POEM

Have you ever watched an honest dance
that nailed your eyes to the edge of the grave?
You're free to chew the dead's skin and flesh

Upright ruins, under the country's flag pole,
bring you, and I mean all of you,
to carnal desires.

Rumbling dust
roaring lust:
you call me stupid

This is the country of May, amoi!
The dragon dance swerves in red throughout the city
You wave the bra right under the two-colored flag,
red and white.
Like blood. Like skin.
"Let's roast the satay, from the cry of the virgin who hasn't finished grade school."
Then you respond humbly,
by plundering the city tunnels
while singing together: All For Country.

CONTRIBUTORS

Zubaidah Djohar is a researcher, trainer, humanitarian activist and a poet. She has published on wide range of issues related to women and the conflict in Aceh. She has worked for projects that seek to empower women, addressing cross-cutting themes of anti-corruption, gender equality, environmental sustainability, and peace building. In her book of poems on women and peace in Aceh, *PULANG Melawan Lupa*, 2012 (English Version: *Building a Boat in Paradise*, translated by Heather Curnow, 2014), she raises the importance of remembering the violence and the suffering of the conflict survivors, especially women and children, as a path towards reconciliation. She dedicated the revenues of her poetry books for the recovery of the conflict victims.

Shinta Febriany was born in South Sulawesi, Indonesia. She is the Artistic Director of Kala Teater, based in Makassar, South Sulawesi. In 2007 Shinta was awarded Celebes Award from South Sulawesi Provincial Government for her dedication to theater. Shinta graduated from the Theater and Visual Art Studies programme at the Gadjah Mada University Graduate School. As a theater director, playwright, and poet Shinta's works are known for challenging gender stereotypes, exploring embodiment, and examining contemporary urban problems in East Indonesia.

Hanna Fransisca was born in Singkawang, West Kalimantan, in 1979. Her writings have appeared in major media in Indonesia. Her poetry collections are *Konde Penyair Han* (2010), *Benih Dewa Dapur* (2012), and *A man Bathing and Other Poems,* a trilingual book in German, English, and Indonesian (2015). She has also published a short story collection *Sulaiman Pergi ke Tanjung Cina* (2012) and a play, *Kawan Tidur* (Sleeping Buddies, 2012), translated into English and published in *New Indonesian Plays* (Aurora Metro Books, 2019). *Konde Penyair Han* was selected as Best Poetry Collection by *Tempo* Magazine in 2011. In 2016, she was invited to Germany to participate in Frankfurt Book Fair and Schamrock Festival der Dichterinnen 2016.

Eliza Vitri Handayani is a novelist, creator of art events, and literary translator. Writing in Indonesian and English, her original works have appeared in many Indonesian and international literary outlets. Her novel *From Now On Everything Will Be Different* (2015) earned her a WrICE fellowship (2016) and invitations to various festivals. She is the founding director of InterSastra, an independent initiative for barrier-breaking creative exploration and exchange. Eliza has translated writers from Indonesia and other countries, and created House of the Unsilenced and Fashion ForWords art events. Eliza is a member of As-Salam Collective and an Australia Arts Council's International Arts Leader 2019. Read some of her works at elizavitri.com, and greet her on Instagram or Twitter @elizavitri.

Toeti Heraty, born in Bandung, 27 November 1933, is known as an influential poet and professor of philosophy in Indonesia. One of the earliest Indonesian feminist thinkers, she has written poetry, essays, and academic works on women's issues. Her poems have been translated into English, German, Dutch, French, Japanese, Bulgarian, Korean, and Italian. She has established many important cultural initiatives in Indonesia and received awards from the governments of Indonesia, Netherlands and France. She has been invited to Poetry International Rotterdam, Iowa International Writers Program, International Literatuurfestival Winternachten in Den Haag, Poetry International SOAS and Poetry Translation Centre in London, and many other international events.

Dorothea Rosa Herliany writes poetry, short stories, children's books, biography, and novels. Her latest book of poetry was bilingual, in German and Indonesian: *Der Messer Hochzeit / Nikah Pisau* (translated by: Brigitte Oleschinski and Ulrike Draesner, Verlagshaus Berlin, 2015). She had worked as a publisher of literary books for more than ten years. She is the recipient of several literary awards, including the Khatulistiwa Literary Award for her poetry book *Santa Rosa* (2006) and for her novel *Isinga, Roman Papua* (2015).

Intan Paramaditha is an Indonesian writer and an academic based in Sydney. She is the author of *Apple and Knife* (2018), a collection of short stories about disobedient women published in Australia and the UK. Her novel *Gentayangan* was selected as *Tempo* Best Literary Fiction of 2017 and translated by Stephen J. Epstein as *The Wandering* (Harvill Secker 2020). It received a PEN Translates Award from the English PEN and PEN/Heim Translation Fund Grant from PEN America. She holds a Ph.D. from New York University and teaches media and film studies at Macquarie University.

Norman Erikson Pasaribu is an Indonesian writer, editor, and translator. Tiffany Tsao's English translation of his book of poems *Sergius Seeks Bacchus*, winner of a PEN Translates Award, is out in the UK with Tilted Axis. Norman won the Young Author Award from the Southeast Asia Literary Council, and his poem was nominated for the 2020 Rhysling Award. He lives in Bekasi with his family and their two cats and a swan.

Tiffany Tsao is a writer and literary translator. She is the author of the novel *The Majesties* (originally published in Australia as *Under Your Wings*) and the *Oddfits* fantasy series. Her translations from Indonesian to English include Norman Erikson Pasaribu's poetry collection *Sergius Seeks Bacchus*, Dee Lestari's novel *Paper Boats,* and Laksmi Pamuntjak's *The Birdwoman's Palate*. Her translations of Norman's poetry have won the English PEN Presents and English PEN Translates awards. she holds a Ph.D. in English literature from UC-Berkeley. She now lives in Sydney, Australia with her spouse and two children.

Copyright
© Toeti Heraty, Dorothea Rosa Herliany, Zubaidah Djohar, Shinta Febriany, and Hanna Fransisca 2020
Translations copyright © Tiffany Tsao, Norman Erikson Pasaribu, and Eliza Vitri Handayani 2020
Introduction copyright © Intan Paramaditha 2020

This edition published in the United Kingdom by Tilted Axis Press in 2020. This translation was funded by Arts Council England and 198 brilliant Kickstarter backers. Thank you!

tiltedaxispress.com

The rights of the authors and translators of these works to be identified as such have been asserted in accordance with Section 77 of the Copyright, Designs and Patent Act 1988.

This is a work of fiction. Names, characters, places and incidents are either the product of the author's imagination or are used fictitiously. Any resemblance to any actual persons, living or dead, events or locales is entirely coincidental.

ISBN (chapbook)   9781911284543
ISBN (ebook)   9781911284536

A catalogue record for this book is available from the British Library.

Edited by Intan Paramaditha
Cover design by Soraya Gilanni Viljoen
Typesetting and ebook production by Simon Collinson
Printed and bound by Footprint Workers Co-op, Leeds

Supported using public funding by
ARTS COUNCIL ENGLAND